MW01139574

JAN -- 2023

COUNTRY 🌐 PROFILES

NEW ZEALAND

BY ALICIA Z. KLEPEIS

BLASTOFF!
DISCOVERY

BELLWETHER MEDIA • MINNEAPOLIS, MN

Blastoff! Discovery launches a new mission: reading to learn. Filled with facts and features, each book offers you an exciting new world to explore!

BLASTOFF! UNIVERSE

BLASTOFF! Beginners — GRADE K

BLASTOFF! READERS — GRADES 1-3

BLASTOFF! DISCOVERY — GRADE 4

This edition first published in 2021 by Bellwether Media, Inc.

No part of this publication may be reproduced in whole or in part without written permission of the publisher.
For information regarding permission, write to Bellwether Media, Inc.,
Attention: Permissions Department,
6012 Blue Circle Drive, Minnetonka, MN 55343.

Library of Congress Cataloging-in-Publication Data
Names: Klepeis, Alicia, 1971- author.
Title: New Zealand / Alicia Z. Klepeis.
Description: Minneapolis, MN : Bellwether Media, Inc., [2021]
  | Series: Blastoff! Discovery: country profiles | Includes
  bibliographical references and index.
Audience: Ages 7-13 | Audience: Grades 4-6 | Summary: "Engaging
  images accompany information about New Zealand. The combination
  of high-interest subject matter and narrative text is intended for students
  in grades 3 through 8"– Provided by publisher.
Identifiers: LCCN 2020049055 (print) | LCCN 2020049056 (ebook)
  | ISBN 9781644874516 (library binding)
  | ISBN 9781648341281 (ebook)
Subjects: LCSH: New Zealand–Juvenile literature.
Classification: LCC DU408 .K55 2021 (print) | LCC DU408 (ebook)
  | DDC 993–dc23
LC record available at https://lccn.loc.gov/2020049055
LC ebook record available at https://lccn.loc.gov/2020049056

Editor: Kieran Downs   Designer: Laura Sowers

Printed in the United States of America, North Mankato, MN.

TABLE OF CONTENTS

REDWOODS
TREEWALK

A family arrives in Rotorua on a damp morning.
They wander through the treetops at the Redwoods Treewalk.
A huge patch of silver ferns lies below them. Next, the family
takes a lunch cruise around Lake Rotorua. They stop to see
the bird **sanctuary** at Mokoia Island.

OTHER TOP SITES

BAY OF ISLANDS

HOBBITON

MILFORD SOUND

TONGARIRO NATIONAL PARK

In the late afternoon, they visit nearby Waimangu **Volcanic** Valley. The waters of Inferno Crater Lake are a brilliant shade of blue. Colorful kereru birds beat their wings noisily as they fly by. Before bed, the family soaks in the hot springs at their hotel. Welcome to New Zealand!

WONDERFUL WELLINGTON

Wellington is the world's southernmost national capital. Most people in the city live within 1.9 miles (3 kilometers) of the sea. The city has over 226 miles (364 kilometers) of walking and mountain bike trails.

AUCKLAND

HAMILTON

TAURANGA

TASMAN SEA

WELLINGTON

COOK STRAIT

CHRISTCHURCH

NEW ZEALAND

PACIFIC OCEAN

New Zealand is a nation in the South Pacific Ocean. This island country covers 103,799 square miles (268,838 square kilometers). New Zealand has hundreds of islands. The North and South Islands are its two largest. The Cook **Strait** separates them.

Wellington is the capital of New Zealand. It is located on the southern tip of the North Island. New Zealand does not border any other countries. Australia lies about 1,000 miles (1,600 kilometers) to the northwest across the Tasman Sea. New Zealand's other neighbors include Fiji, Tonga, and New Caledonia. These islands are all north of New Zealand in the South Pacific Ocean.

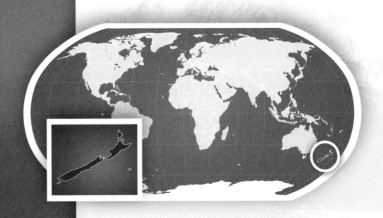

LANDSCAPE AND CLIMATE

The North Island of New Zealand has hot springs, **fertile** land, and a rocky coastline. Several active volcanoes are located in the Taupo Volcanic Zone. This area cuts into the center of the island.

The Southern Alps run the length of the South Island. **Glaciers** are found in these mountains. To the east, the Canterbury **Plains** feature miles of farmland. Deep glacial lakes and **fjords** are also part of the South Island's landscape.

= TAUPO VOLCANIC ZONE
= SOUTHERN ALPS

TAUPO VOLCANIC ZONE

WELLINGTON
Average seasonal highs and lows

JANUARY
HIGH 70 °F (21 °C)
LOW 58 °F (14 °C)

APRIL
HIGH 62 °F (17 °C)
LOW 52 °F (11 °C)

JULY
HIGH 53 °F (12 °C)
LOW 44 °F (7 °C)

OCTOBER
HIGH 59 °F (15 °C)
LOW 49 °F (9 °C)

°F = degrees Fahrenheit
°C = degrees Celsius

RING OF FIRE

New Zealand is located on the Pacific Ring of Fire. As a result, New Zealand often has earthquakes. Most of the time, however, they are minor.

Overall, New Zealand has a **temperate** climate. On the coasts, temperatures are mostly mild. Temperatures are often cooler in the mountains. Rain falls throughout the year.

9

WILDLIFE

Because of its island location, New Zealand is home to many animals found nowhere else in the world. Tuataras are lizard-like reptiles that only live on the offshore islands of New Zealand. They feed on spiders and giant insects called wētās. Bats are the nation's only **native** land mammals. New Zealand fur seals dive for fish in the waters along the coastlines.

New Zealand is also known for its birds. Tuis and bellbirds flit about in the nation's forests. Flightless kiwi birds poke around on the forest floor for seeds, grubs, and worms. Yellow-eyed penguins live along the country's southeastern coast and surrounding islands.

GIANT WĒTĀ

TUATARA

TUI

NEW ZEALAND FUR SEAL

A BOLD PLAN

Most of New Zealand's bird species are at risk of becoming extinct. To help save them, the country has a plan to get rid of all non-native predator animals by 2050.

10

NORTHERN BROWN KIWI

NORTHERN BROWN KIWI

Life Span: 20 years
Red List Status: vulnerable

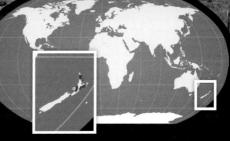

northern brown kiwi range =

LEAST CONCERN	NEAR THREATENED	VULNERABLE	ENDANGERED	CRITICALLY ENDANGERED	EXTINCT IN THE WILD	EXTINCT

New Zealand is home to around 5 million people.
New Zealanders are also called Kiwis. Nearly two-thirds
have European **ancestors**. Many came from Great Britain.
The second-largest group of people is the Māori. They likely
settled in New Zealand during the 13th century, after traveling
from Polynesia. Many Pacific Islanders and Asian **immigrants**,
such as Chinese and Indians, call New Zealand home.

Nearly half of the people in New Zealand follow no religion. About one out of every three are Christians. Nearly all Kiwis speak English. English, Māori, and New Zealand Sign Language are all official languages.

FAMOUS FACE

Name: **Lorde**
(born Ella Marija Lani Yelich-O'Connor)
Birthday: **November 7, 1996**
Hometown: **Takapuna, Auckland, New Zealand**
Famous for: **Award-winning singer-songwriter who won two Grammy Awards while still in high school**

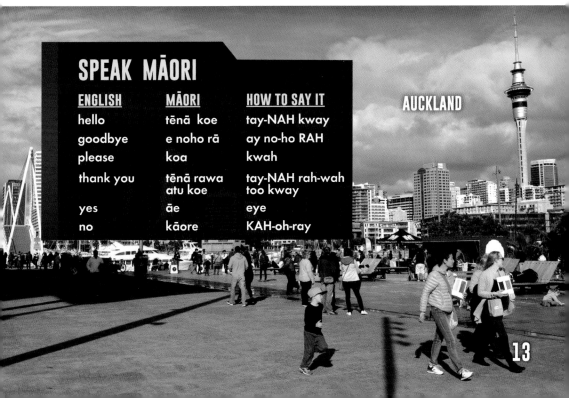

SPEAK MĀORI

ENGLISH	MĀORI	HOW TO SAY IT
hello	tēnā koe	tay-NAH kway
goodbye	e noho rā	ay no-ho RAH
please	koa	kwah
thank you	tēnā rawa atu koe	tay-NAH rah-wah too kway
yes	āe	eye
no	kāore	KAH-oh-ray

AUCKLAND

More than 8 out of 10 Kiwis live in **urban** areas.
Most of them live on the North Island. The nation's largest
city, Auckland, is home to over 1.6 million people. Many city
dwellers live in apartments. Others have single-family homes.
Buses, trains, and **ferries** are all ways people get around.
People also drive their own cars.

FERRY
AUCKLAND

Life in the countryside has a slower pace. The cost of living is cheaper than in the cities. Driving is often the most common way to get around in **rural** areas.

CUSTOMS

JACINDA ARDERN

In 2018, New Zealand's prime minister Jacinda Ardern gave birth to a baby. She is only the second world leader in history to do so while holding office.

New Zealanders are known for being quite friendly and relaxed. It is common for friends or family members to drop by each other's homes unannounced. They are more likely to chat about activities or family rather than work or money.

The arts are an important part of Māori **culture**. One example of this is the *haka*. This **traditional** dance involves powerful moves, shouts, and facial expressions. Haka dances are performed at weddings and birthdays. Other popular Māori arts include wood and bone carving.

HAKA DANCERS

TRAVEL THE WORLD

After high school or college, Kiwis often go on an Overseas Experience. During this time, they work in other countries and learn about different cultures.

Students in New Zealand are required to attend school between the ages of 6 and 16. Primary school lasts eight years. Some schools teach classes in Māori. Students then go to five years of secondary school. New Zealand is also home to several universities.

Over 7 out of 10 Kiwis have **service jobs**. Some work in schools, hospitals, or on construction sites. In 2019, around 3.8 million people visited New Zealand. The travelers provided many jobs in **tourism**. New Zealand factories produce paper, **textiles**, and building materials. Farmers grow barley, wheat, and fruits and vegetables. They also raise sheep and cattle.

TOURISM

SHEEP FARMER

RUGBY

NETBALL

Sports are wildly popular among New Zealanders. The national sport is rugby. The All Blacks national team has won the Rugby World Cup many times. Soccer and cricket are well-liked, too. Netball and basketball are also popular sports.

Common outdoor activities include hiking, fishing, and sailing. Bungee jumping is a popular adventure sport that was invented in New Zealand. Whitewater rafting is another exciting activity, as is black water rafting in underground caves. Gardening is a more relaxing popular hobby. New Zealanders also travel frequently.

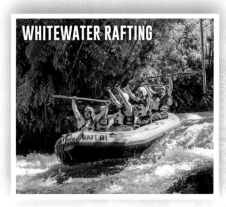
WHITEWATER RAFTING

MAKE A MĀORI NECKLACE

A traditional Māori activity is carving. Necklaces made of whalebone or greenstone are prized. Commonly used designs include the fish hook, ground fern, or twist. Create your own Māori necklace!

What You Need:
- air-dry clay
- green paint and paintbrush (optional)
- pencil or toothpick
- leather cord or string

Instructions:
1. Check out some images of Māori carved necklaces either online or in a book.
2. Take a golf-ball-sized piece of clay. Roll it into a sausage shape.
3. For the fern shape, make a loose spiral from your piece of clay. For the twist necklace, twist the sausage shape of clay so that it forms two or three small loops. After you make the design you want, flatten the clay with the palm of your hand.
4. Use a pencil or toothpick to create a hole near the top of your design.
5. Let the clay air dry completely. If desired, paint your necklace green and let dry.
6. Thread your cord or string through the hole, and tie a knot at the end. Have fun wearing your new necklace!

HOKEY POKEY

Hokey pokey is a beloved ice cream flavor in New Zealand. It is vanilla ice cream with small chunks of honeycomb toffee mixed in.

Kiwis eat a lot of seafood thanks to New Zealand's huge coastline. Fish-and-chips is a popular dish. Crayfish and sea urchins, called *kina*, are also well-liked. Roasted lamb is a favorite dish for many people. One Māori food tradition is *hangi*. Meat, seafood, vegetables, and sweet potatoes, called *kumara*, are slow-roasted in an underground oven for hours.

Many kinds of fruit grow in New Zealand. Passionfruit, boysenberries, and kiwis are just a few examples. Cheese is very popular throughout the country. Lemon & Paeroa, known as L&P by locals, is a sweet soda that was invented in New Zealand in 1904.

KINA

KUMARA

PAVLOVA

Pavlova is one of New Zealand's best-known desserts. Have an adult help you make it.

Ingredients:
4 egg whites
1 1/4 cups sugar
pinch of salt
1 teaspoon lemon juice
1 teaspoon vanilla extract
2 teaspoons cornstarch
whipped cream
1 pint of berries
6 kiwis, peeled and sliced

Steps:
1. Preheat the oven to 300 degrees Fahrenheit (149 degrees Celsius). Line a baking sheet with parchment paper. Use a pencil to roughly draw a 9-inch (23-centimeter) circle on the paper.

2. In a big bowl, beat the egg whites until stiff. This should take several minutes. Gradually add in the sugar, about 1 tablespoon at a time. Add in a pinch of salt.

3. Gently mix in the cornstarch, lemon juice, and vanilla extract.

4. Spoon the mixture onto the circle marked on the parchment paper. Bake for about 50 to 55 minutes.

5. When cool, serve with berries, kiwi, and whipped cream. Enjoy!

CELEBRATIONS

Kiwis love to celebrate their history.
Waitangi Day takes place on February 6.
It marks the 1840 signing of New Zealand's
founding document, the Treaty of Waitangi.
Typical activities include picnics, kite flying,
and eating traditional Māori food. Anzac Day
is April 25. This holiday shows respect for
all New Zealanders who have served in the
armed forces.

Christmas is usually warm in New Zealand.
People often head to the beach or have a
barbeque. On Boxing Day, December 26,
Kiwis give small gifts to service workers or
donate money to those in need.
New Zealanders celebrate their country
and culture throughout the year!

WAITANGI DAY

A CANDY RACE

Once a year, Kiwis roll about 75,000 chocolate-orange candies called Jaffas down Dunedin's super-steep Baldwin Street. The candies are marked with numbers and winners get prizes. The event raises money for charity.

ANNUAL JAFFA RACE

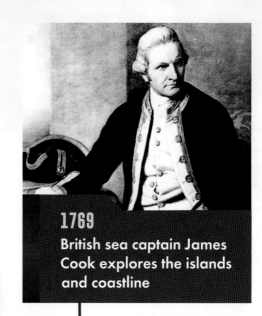

1769
British sea captain James Cook explores the islands and coastline

13TH CENTURY
The Māori people arrive in what is now New Zealand

1840
The Treaty of Waitangi is signed between the Māori and British

1642
Dutch explorer Abel Tasman arrives in New Zealand

1893
New Zealand is the first country in the world to give women the right to vote

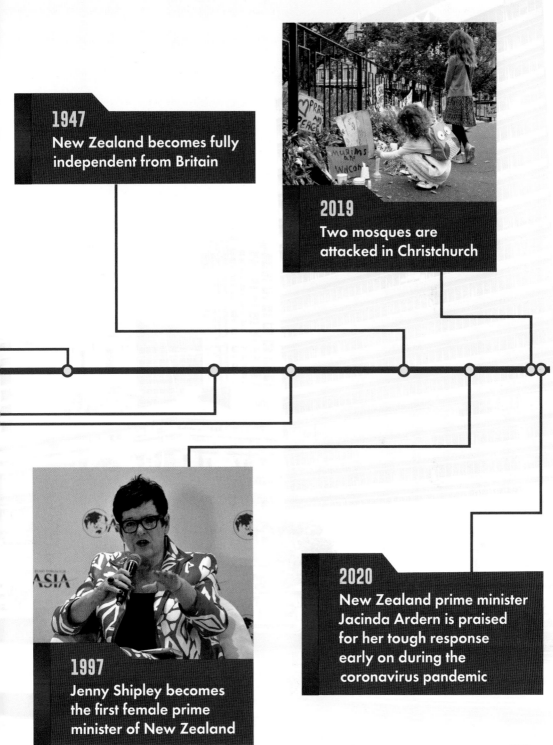

1947
New Zealand becomes fully independent from Britain

2019
Two mosques are attacked in Christchurch

1997
Jenny Shipley becomes the first female prime minister of New Zealand

2020
New Zealand prime minister Jacinda Ardern is praised for her tough response early on during the coronavirus pandemic

27

NEW ZEALAND FACTS

Official Name: New Zealand/Aotearoa (Māori)

Flag of New Zealand: The background of the New Zealand flag is royal blue. The flag of Great Britain, known as the Union Jack, is in the upper left corner. It recognizes New Zealand's time as a British colony. Four red stars of the Southern Cross constellation are on the right side of the flag. They are reminders of the nation's location in the South Pacific Ocean.

Area: 103,799 square miles
(268,838 square kilometers)

Capital City: Wellington

Important Cities: Auckland, Christchurch, Hamilton, Tauranga

Population:
4,925,477 (2020 est.)

COUNTRYSIDE
13.3%

WHERE
PEOPLE LIVE

CITY
86.7%

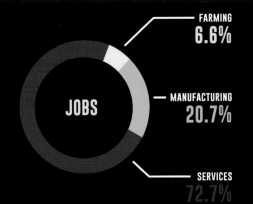

FARMING
6.6%

MANUFACTURING
20.7%

SERVICES
72.7%

JOBS

Main Exports:

wood

beef

aluminum

sheep and
goat meat

dairy
products

fruit

National Holidays:
Waitangi Day (February 6),
Anzac Day (April 25)

Main Languages:
English, Māori,
New Zealand Sign Language

Form of Government:
parliamentary democracy under a
constitutional monarchy

Title for Country Leaders:
prime minister (head of government), queen (chief of state)

RELIGION

CHRISTIAN
37.3%

OTHER
12%

HINDU
2.7%

NO RELIGION
48%

Unit of Money:
New Zealand dollar

GLOSSARY

ancestors—relatives who lived long ago

barbeque—a meal or gathering where meat or other food is cooked outdoors on a grill or over an open fire

culture—the beliefs, arts, and ways of life in a place or society

ferries—boats that carry people or things across water

fertile—able to support growth

fjords—long, deep inlets of a sea that are lined by mountains

glaciers—massive sheets of ice that cover large areas of land

immigrants—people who move to a new country

native—originally from the area or related to animals originally from the area

plains—large areas of flat land

rural—related to the countryside

sanctuary—a place that provides protection or shelter

service jobs—jobs that perform tasks for people or businesses

strait—a narrow channel connecting two larger bodies of water

temperate—associated with a mild climate that does not have extreme heat or cold

textiles—fabrics that are woven or knit

tourism—the business of people traveling to visit other places

traditional—related to customs, ideas, or beliefs handed down from one generation to the next

urban—related to cities and city life

volcanic—related to holes in the earth called volcanoes; when a volcano erupts, hot ash, gas, or melted rock called lava shoots out.

TO LEARN MORE

AT THE LIBRARY

Gitlin, Marty. *Australia*. Minneapolis, Minn.: Bellwether Media, 2018.

McCartney, Tania. *A Kiwi Year: Twelve Months in the Life of New Zealand's Kids.* Gosford, AU: EK Books, 2017.

Smelt, Roselynn. *New Zealand*. New York, N.Y.: Cavendish Square Publishing, 2018.

ON THE WEB

FACTSURFER

Factsurfer.com gives you a safe, fun way to find more information.

1. Go to www.factsurfer.com.

2. Enter "New Zealand" into the search box and click Q.

3. Select your book cover to see a list of related content.

INDEX

The images in this book are reproduced through the courtesy of: 1tomm, cover; RomanSlavik.com, pp. 4-5; DmitrySerbin, p. 5 (Bay of Islands); Blue Planet Studio, p. 5 (Hobbiton, Milford Sound); Dmitry Pichugin, pp. 5 (Tongariro National Park), 9; 4 season backpacking, p. 8; Victor Maschek, p. 9 (Wellington); Kim Howell, p. 10 (giant weta); Ross Gordon Henry, p. 10 (tuatara); FiledIMAGE, p. 10 (tui); Ryan Fletcher, p. 10 (New Zealand fur seal); Jiri Prochazka, pp. 10-11; Artazum, p. 12; PictureLux/ The Hollywood Archive/ Alamy Stock Photo, p. 13 (top); ChameleonsEye, pp. 13 (bottom), 18, 27 (top); eye35/ Alamy Stock Photo, p. 14; S Curtis, p. 15; lev radin, p. 16; travelstock44/ Alamy Stock Photo, p. 17; Boyloso, p. 19 (top); Carpe Diem - New Zealand/ Alamy Stock Photo, p. 19 (bottom); Mai Groves, p. 20 (top); Chris Hellyar, p. 20 (bottom); rodcoffee, p. 21 (top); CreativeFireStock, p. 21 (bottom); LazingBee/ Getty Images, p. 22; eclecticworks, p. 23 (kina); nazar_ab, p. 23 (kumara); bonchan, p. 23 (pavlova); paul kennedy/ Alamy Stock Photo, p. 24; Rob Jefferies/ Stringer, pp. 24-25; Everett Collection, p. 26 (top); National Library of Australia/ Wikipedia, p. 26 (bottom); Imaginechina Limite/ Alamy Stock Photo, p. 27 (bottom); Jennifer Gottschalk, p. 29 (banknote); Ben Jeayes, p. 29 (coin).